MALLARD PRESS

An imprint of BDD Promotional Books Company, Inc.,
666 Fifth Avenue, New York, N.Y. 10103

Mallard Press and its accompanying design and logo
are trademarks of BDD Promotional Book Company, Inc.

CLB 2342
Copyright © 1990 Colour Library Books Ltd.,
Godalming, Surrey, England.
Copyright © 1990 Illustrations: Oxford Scientific Films Ltd.,
Long Hanborough, England.
First published in the United States of America
in 1990 by The Mallard Press
Printed and bound in Italy by Fratelli Spada, SpA
All rights reserved.
ISBN 0 792 45029 9

· Oxford Scientific Films ·

BEARS

Michael Leach

MALLARD
PRESS

Contents

*Previous page: a tree provides a safe place
for this black bear to sleep while away from
its den. These pages: meadows are perfect
feeding grounds when the plants are young
and tender.*

1

What is a Bear?

A bear is a fascinating animal. It belongs to one of the most powerful *species* on earth, It eats almost anything, and can survive in a wide variety of *habitats*. Bears were once very common before humans started to hunt them. The grizzly or brown bear once lived throughout North America, northern Asia and Europe, but they became *extinct* in Britain during the tenth century. The American black bear used to be found all over Canada, America and Mexico, but now they live mainly in national parks and wilderness areas.

The bear's most important sense is that of smell. Bears search for food and are alerted to danger by using their sensitive noses, constantly sniffing the ground and air to tell them what is happening nearby. Relatively poor eyesight and hearing make the bear's nose a particularly important sensory organ. Being short-sighted, the animal does not always recognize danger until it is very close, and then it rears up to make itself look bigger. This is usually enough to frighten off most enemies, as a fully grown grizzly on its hind legs stands almost nine feet high. However, the biggest species of bear in the world is the polar bear, and that can stand up to ten feet.

Bears can walk only a few steps on their hind legs and this usually only happens when they attack. On all four legs, they have a bow-legged, clumsy way of moving that usually makes them slow, yet they can move surprisingly fast: a grizzly has been timed running at 31 miles per hour. Everyone knows stories of famous bear

Common in the unspoilt wilderness of Alaska, the brown bear is an expert fisher.

The flat, round feet of the bear help to spread the weight of its enormously heavy body. The Alaskan brown bear (above) is among the largest of all bears. Koalas (left) are not bears at all. They are Australian marsupials and are related to the kangaroo.

hugs, where enemies are crushed to death, but in fact bears only "hug" when they play, although an attacking bear hits its enemies with both front paws and, at a distance, this could look like hugging.

The word "bear" is often used to describe animals that are not even related to true bears. The koala of Australia is a marsupial that was given the name bear just because of its physical similarity to a bear. Pandas appear to be black and white bears, but in fact they belong to the raccoon family. By contrast, the mythical yeti or abominable snowman of the Himalayas might just turn out to be a bear living high in the mountains.

2

Bears of the World

There are no bears at all in Africa, Australia or the Antarctic – in fact, apart from the South American spectacled bear, all bears live in the northern hemisphere.

The grizzly or brown bear is the most widespread of bears and can be found in Europe, Asia and North America. Though once common, they are now becoming increasingly rare, and the European bears are in danger of disappearing altogether. The biggest grizzlies live in Siberia and Alaska and are known as Kodiak bears.

The American black bear is smaller than the grizzly and lives only in America and Canada. These secretive and intelligent bears still survive in large numbers, especially in national parks and undisturbed forests, and they can become a problem when they learn to raid dustbins in search of food.

The polar bear is the biggest species of bear, and the largest land *carnivore* in the world. These giant bears live only in the Arctic, but unlike other species they regularly travel vast distances – primarily to avoid the harsh winters of the northern Arctic. Few plants can survive in this habitat, so the polar bear's main food is meat.

The spectacled bear is the only bear in South America and it lives around the northern part of the Andes mountains. This animal gets its name from the ring of light fur around each of its eyes. These markings are always slightly different, so no two spectacled bears look exactly the same.

The sloth bear lives in India and Sri Lanka. these shaggy-coated animal has a longer nose than any other bear, its two top *incisor teeth* are missing and it can even open and close its nostrils at will. A young sloth bear sometimes travels on its mother's back, something that no other bear does.

The sun bear is the smallest member of the bear family and it lives on the southeast tip of Asia and on the Indonesian islands of Borneo and Sumatra. Although they are not likely to attack, sun bears are often killed by the local farmers who think, wrongly, that they are dangerous.

The Asian black bear lives over most of Asia, from Iran to Japan. It gets its scientific name of Selenarctos, which means moon bear, from the new-moon-shaped patches of white fur on its chest. The rest of its coat is black and, in sunlight, looks almost purple.

Short hair helps to keep the Malayan sun bear (facing page) cool in its warm environment. Polar bear cubs (above) stay with their mother for about two years, relying on her for food until they are able to kill for themselves. Right: the spectacled bear of South America.

3
Life of Bears

Bears are not sociable animals. They do not get along with each other and usually only come together during the breeding season, or at places where food is plentiful. When bears meet, the smaller usually runs off before it is attacked. If the two are evenly matched they will often fight, each trying to drive the other away. As a result of their size and strength, adult bears have no natural enemies, apart from man, and they can live for up to thirty years in the wild.

As smell is their most important sense, light is not important to bears. Most species are *nocturnal* and spend their days dozing in one of many resting places inside their *territory*, but all seven species are known to be active during some daylight hours. In hot conditions they like to stay close to water. All bears can swim, but much of their time is spent playing on their own – they splash, roll and even dive into waterholes and rivers. Regular bathing cleans the bears' fur and helps keep down the number of fleas.

The humped back (above) is a characteristic of the brown bear (these pages). As well as helping to keep them free of fleas, playing in water (right) is a pastime many bears enjoy.

During the summer months, bears get hot and are bothered by clouds of flies that drone around them. Like other animals, they like to scratch to ease the bites left by annoying insects, but they can't use their short, stiff legs, so instead they rub themselves against hard objects, such as trees. Some trees are used so much that they are known as "bear-trees," and these are distinguishable by the thick tufts of hair left at their base by an itchy bear which has scratched and scraped itself against the rough bark.

During the night's feeding, bears move slowly, stopping every few minutes to look for food or to sniff the air for scents of possible danger. They rarely wander more than five miles in one night, and some bear trails have been used for hundreds of years; they usually lead to good feeding grounds or favorite pools. Centuries of wear by the bears' big, heavy feet stops everything

Although bears rarely fight, an encounter between males during the breeding season can result in injury, or even death.

growing along the path and sometimes even forms a faint groove where the soil is packed down hard by their enormous weight.

The size of a bear's territory depends on how much food is available and how many other bears there are nearby. In Alaska, female grizzlies cover over five-and-a-half square miles, but in Alberta, Canada, they range over 73 square miles. Bear territories do not overlap very much and trespassers of the same sex are soon driven out. Males range over a much larger area than females. There may be two or three females, each with her own territory, inside an area covered by a single male.

4

Food

Bears are *omnivores*, which means that they will eat almost anything. Apart from the polar bear, which is almost entirely carnivorous, the diet of bears includes such things as grasses, nuts, berries, fish and meat. Being so big, they need a large amount of food; a grizzly bear eats up to 35 pounds a day, though the smaller sun bear eats just thirteen pounds. Sloth bears enjoy eating termites and have developed a good technique for reaching them. Termites live in mounds of sand set like concrete by the insects' saliva. The sloth bear cracks open the mound with its claws and uses its rubbery lips and long tongue first to blow away the dust and then to suck up the termites. A hungry bear will sit for hours carefully sucking tiny insects out of their tunnels.

Bears love sweet food and will eagerly attack bee colonies to feed off the sweet, rich honey inside the hive. In North America the black bear often raids hives, smashing them to get at the

honey, while its thick coat protects it from the sting of angry bees defending their colony. This destructive behaviour of the bears annoys bee-keepers, but it is difficult to keep these animals out of anywhere when they are determined to get in.

All bears will eat meat whenever they can. Most of this comes in the form of insects and grubs, but they will also dig up mice and other small animals from underground nests. Large species, like the grizzly and Asian black bear, even kill *prey* as big as deer. On farmland they will sometimes attack sheep and young cattle. Each of the bear's paws is armed with five sharp, curved claws, and a couple of powerful blows is enough to break the neck, or even the back, of large prey.

Rich pickings are to be had by Alaskan bears during the migration of salmon in the spawning season.

The Malayan sun bear uses its amazingly long tongue to investigate holes and lick up small insects.

When breeding, some species of fish, such as salmon, migrate from the sea into rivers, and often millions fight their way along streams to reach their *spawning grounds*. All the bears have to do is wait for them, catching the fish either by snapping them up with their long canine teeth and strong jaws, or else flipping them out of the water with their front paws. This is easy work, so bears from miles around will visit rivers when there are such fish moving through. The normally solitary bears come into close contact with each other when fishing, and this causes fights, but in the end it is always the strongest animals that get the best part of the river for fishing.

Above: when there are plenty of fish available, bears will eat only the best parts and leave the rest. Bears are omnivorous, generally eating whatever food is readily available, even carrion (facing page).

5

Habitat

Bears are not specialists that live in only one habitat, instead they need a mixture of environments to provide them with a variety of food. Bears particularly like woodland areas; trees supply shelter in bad weather, as well as food such as fruit, berries and leaves. Lots of bears enjoy eating sap from trees, which they reach by biting and scraping away the bark and licking the rich, thick sap underneath. All bears need a good supply of water, since they drink a large amount every day.

In autumn, bears move to areas where the best fruit grows. Even in the Arctic (below), brown bears can find berries growing on low shrubs.

BEARS

Once a bear has found a good territory, it usually stays there for life. It is important for a bear to know one area well, so that it can make good use of the best feeding places. Inside its home range a bear will know where each tree is and exactly when the food it supplies is ready for eating. When the habitats of two species overlap, such as sun bears and black bears in Asia, or grizzlies and black bears in North America, the smaller one is always kept away from the best feeding sites. Different species can share a habitat as long as they keep apart. Since they do not meet often, droppings are used as communication. Each bear has its own scent, so droppings tell visiting bears where other bears are and when they were there. These signs are useful because it has been known for grizzlies to kill black bears when they meet accidentally.

In most areas bears share their habitat with man. This causes problems for the bears as they are frightened of humans, but, at the same time, they are attracted by the food that we keep around us. Hungry bears do sometimes raid

American black bears (facing page top) prefer forests to any other habitat. Here they can find both food and shelter. Above: a brown bear standing on its hind legs to see above the long grass growing on the banks of an Alaskan river.

storehouses, but most of the time they avoid coming close to human settlements. Due to over-hunting and other pressures from man, species like the grizzly and the spectacled bear are now only found in remote wilderness areas, where they can live undisturbed.

Bears' choice of habitat is often controlled by the weather. In spring they like grassy meadows where they graze on young, fresh shoots and dig up roots. During the summer they sometimes move onto the higher ground of nearby hills where the growing season is short, but produces rich vegetation. In early autumn, though, the hills get cold and the first snow appears, forcing the bears to move down to lower ground where it is warmer.

6

The Ice Bear

Polar bears are closely related to grizzlies, but their behavior and habitat are very different. In Scandinavia they are called "ice bears," a suitable name for an animal that lives in places so cold that the sea itself becomes frozen. Everything about the polar bear is adapted to survival in very low temperatures. Their thick, yellow-white fur is the most obvious protection against the cold, while beneath this is skin lined with a dense layer of fat. This insulates them very efficiently – even in a harsh Arctic winter the body temperature of a polar bear is slightly higher than that of a human. Like many other animals living in cold climates, each hair on the polar bear is hollow and filled with air, providing further *insulation* and giving the bear extra buoyancy in water.

There is not much land north of the Arctic Circle, so the habitat of the polar bear is made up mainly of ice and water. These huge bears are surprisingly good swimmers, although they do not look particularly elegant as they move along with their powerful, but slow, dog-paddle movement. There are small webs between each claw of the polar bear's feet, and its coat is covered with an oily grease that keeps it waterproof and stops ice forming on the fur. Polar bears migrate in the spring and autumn, as the sea-ice melts and re-forms with the changing

A polar bear grooming.

Top: female polar bears are very protective of their cubs, guarding them from wolves and even other bears. Powerful swimmers, polar bears (above) have been sighted as much as 200 miles from land.

seasons. They spend much of their lives travelling and can cover huge distances. One bear, studied around the coast of Alaska, moved more than 680 miles in a single year. Most of the *migration* is over water. Bears have been seen swimming more than 200 miles away from the nearest land, and tired polar bears often climb onto floating icebergs that are carried away by the sea currents. During the short summer months in the Arctic many polar bears move onto the tundra to feed on berries, birds' eggs and small mammals.

Polar bears breed in dens dug into deep, drifted snow. The female enters the den in November and the cubs are born in December or January, weighing just under one-and-a-half pounds. They are fed on milk which contains a lot of fat and this helps them to grow very rapidly. Nursery dens are almost impossible to find as the entrance and tracks are soon covered by falling snow. The sleeping bears inside go unnoticed until they dig themselves out in April.

7

The Hunting Bear

Polar bears live mainly on meat. They will hunt for small mammals, fish and even birds, but their main food is seals. There are many species that live in the high Arctic, but polar bears are selective, preferring ringed and bearded seals, and they catch them in several different ways. During the summer months seals are caught by *stalking*. They are slow and clumsy on dry land and never venture far from the safety of the open sea. A bear has to be very skilful in trying to catch a seal lying a few feet from water. The polar bear's coat is perfect *camouflage* and they can move in absolute silence, as their feet are huge and padded, making their footsteps inaudible. Like all hunters, they must use the wind properly. Bears approach their prey from downwind, so ensuring that their scent is carried away from the unsuspecting animal. Even when dozing, seals are aware of the smells around them, but by the time they smell the bear, it is usually too late to escape. The polar bear kills with a powerful blow from a front paw, or a swift bite. They have much longer and sharper teeth than the other species of bear, well-adapted to their diet of meat.

In spring, seals haul themselves out of the water to give birth, and their pups are born in dens dug into the ice. Using their keen sense of smell, polar bears find these dens and dig out the seals inside. The bear's favorite hunting technique needs a lot of patience, but not much effort. Although seals are *aquatic animals*, they still need to breathe air once every ten or fifteen minutes, but thick sea-ice stops them surfacing wherever they want, so they have to use small air-holes, kept ice-free as they are used by up to a dozen seals. The bear finds a breathing hole in the ice and lies very close to it, completely still. When a seal comes up for air the bear strikes and the hunt is over in less than a second.

Polar bears hunt in open sea by diving deep into the water and attacking their prey from underneath. As well as catching seals in this way, they can take the much bigger walrus and even a small whale, like a beluga or pilot whale.

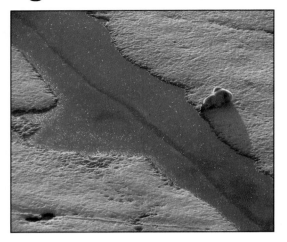

Polar bears will lie for hours beside a breathing hole or crack in the ice (top) waiting for a seal to appear. It is impossible to judge what species a bear belongs to from its color alone. This American black bear (above) has a much lighter coat than the larger brown bear.

Above: brown bears stand above a waterfall simply waiting for migrating salmon to swim into range. Polar bears (left) have been known to swim more than thirty miles in one day.

For centuries polar bears have been hunted by Eskimos and other northern tribes, and, very occasionally, hungry polar bears will attack humans. These huge animals are the supreme *predators* of the Arctic and even man will be looked upon as food if there is nothing else to eat.

8

Bears in Winter

In the tropics there is little difference between the seasons, and fruit and nuts grow all year round, so there is plenty of food available. However, in the colder, northern countries winter makes survival difficult for most animals. Growing thick, warm coats, bears are not bothered by cold weather, but in the long winter there is nothing for them to eat. American and Asian black bears and grizzlies have solved the problem of winter by sleeping all the way through it.

Bears do not go into true *hibernation* like bats or dormice, because their body temperature and heart rate does not change very much. The bears' winter is just spent in very deep sleep, although they can easily be woken by noises or changes in temperature. This behavior is called "denning." They will go to sleep anywhere that is quiet and well protected from the weather. They choose hollow logs, caves or crevices between rocks, and will usually use the same den year after year. The length of the sleep depends on the weather. Grizzly bears in northern Canada will often sleep for up to six months a year because the winters there are very long, but grizzlies in America, where the winters are shorter, only sleep for two or three months.

Inside its warm winter den, a sleeping black bear uses little energy and does not need to eat. Bears may return to the same den year after year.

To make their dens warm and comfortable, bears prepare them in the autumn, lining them with grass or leaves (above). Brown bears (left) dig their winter dens in areas that are dry, quiet and sheltered.

Bears get through winter by eating huge amounts in autumn before they move into their dens. For a month before denning they will spend all their time eating. In just a few weeks a grizzly bear will put on up to 400 pounds extra weight. Inside the dens the bears do not move around so they do not use much energy and the extra fat is enough to see them through even a six-month sleep.

Bears wake up properly when the temperature outside gets warm for more than three or four days. After leaving the den, the first thing they do is take a long drink of water. After several months asleep they need water more than food. For the first week, the newly-woken bears are slow and stiff, and they spend their whole time eating.

9

Park Bears

Facing page: a cinnamon-colored black bear. Above: this American black bear has learned that it is much easier to search through a rubbish tip than to look for food in the woods.

In many national parks, bears have lost their natural fear of man. A Yellowstone National Park sign warns visitors of the dangers.

The closest most people ever get to a wild bear is in a reserve where the wildlife is fully protected. The most famous bear reserve is Yellowstone National Park in Wyoming. The park was created in 1872, and all hunting was banned there from the beginning. Over this hundred-year period the bears have lost their fear of man and have started to see him as a supplier of food. Every year there are over two million visitors to the park and they all want to see its most famous inhabitants.

There are two species of bear in the American parks. The brown or grizzly bear and the black bear. These names are of no help in identification because both species come in assorted colors, from cream to black (there are brown-colored black bears and black-colored brown bears), but their shape is very different. The brown bear is much larger and has a big hump on top of its shoulders. The black bear has a straight nose, while that of the brown bear turns up at the end.

The best way to see an animal close up is to feed it by hand, and the bears were not slow to take advantage when this opportunity was presented to them. Being omnivorous, bears would eat anything offered to them – sandwiches, cake, chocolate, fruit – in fact any picnic food. This was much easier than hunting, so the bears would sit and wait by the roadside or in camp sites until man – and his food – turned up. Most visitors just wanted to look at and photograph the bears, but there were a few who came to tease them. They let the bears see and smell the food, but wouldn't give them any. The bears thought that the food was being stolen and so attacked their "enemy." To stop any further problems between bears and man, the park authorities banned feeding altogether.

Although no one was allowed to feed them, the bears still remembered that humans meant food, so they did not move away. Hungry bears started to raid garbage and rubbish tips and would even break into tents if they could smell food. This was still dangerous to visitors, and the bears had to be stopped. Any bear now found stealing food is darted with a tranquilizer and driven out into the wilderness part of Yellowstone, miles away from camp sites.

10

Breeding

Adult male brown bears (above left) will fight for a female in the breeding season. The loser is always driven away. Above: like all young bears, this grizzly cub seems to have a head that is slightly too big for its body. Facing page: a brown bear mother suckles her cubs.

Like that of most big animals, the bear's breeding cycle is slow – most females only give birth to eight or ten young during their entire lifetime, and female bears do not normally mate until they are around four-and-a-half-years old, while males are usually older. The two sexes stay well away from each other most of the time, coming together only to mate, when males fight each other for the right to mate with females, and only the biggest, fittest males will breed. Sloth and sun bears seem to have just one mate a year, but the other species will mate with several partners during the breeding season.

The two animals stay together for only a few days. After mating the males wander off and have nothing to do with rearing the cubs. The female gives birth about eight months after mating, although sun bear cubs are born after just three months. Grizzlies and black bears mate in the autumn so that the cubs are born in spring, ready to take advantage of the good food supply in summer. As these northern species sleep through the cold weather, the cubs are born in winter dens. Other bears find nursery dens in hollow logs, caves or under tree roots and line them with leaves or grass for warmth.

When the cubs are born they are about the size of rats, and are bald and totally helpless.

The usual number of cubs is two or three, but sometimes there can be four or even five, though in this case they rarely all reach maturity. Cubs stay inside their dens for up to three months, living off their mother's milk, and only when they are strong enough to walk will they venture outside for the first time. Young bears are small and can easily be killed by bigger animals, such as mountain lions or tigers, so they stay close to their mother while they grow and learn. She shows them how to hunt, where to find fruit, which roots to dig up and everything else that they will need to survive. If anything attacks the cubs, the female bear defends them immediately.

The cubs of grizzlies and black bears spend their first winter together in a den with their mother, but after that they find one of their own close to hers. Once the cubs are three years old, they are big enough to look after themselves and so are driven away by the female. Shortly afterwards she mates again and has another *litter* of cubs the following year.

11
Bears in Trees

Bears feel at home in forests and have evolved perfectly for a life among trees. Apart from grizzlies and polar bears, which are too heavy to scale trees, bears are swift and agile climbers. First they reach up and hold the trunk tightly with their front paws, while their back legs grip the trunk and push up at the same time, and then the back legs hold on while the front paws reach up again. In this way a bear can climb the highest tree.

If a bear attacks, it is helpful to know what species it is. Faced with a grizzly, one solution is to climb a nearby tree, but if a black bear charges it is important to remember that they can climb a lot faster than you can.

The spectacled bear lives in a variety of habitats, but it seems to prefer *cloud forest,* where the air is always damp and the vegetation is rich and thick. These bears are not easy to study because they spend a lot of their time in the tree tops. Not much grows on the forest floor as most of the daylight is cut off by the huge trees, so young leaves and the best fruit are found high above ground level. Spectacled bears have no difficulty in getting up trees, but their weight stops them from climbing onto small branches. Like all tree-climbing bears, they sit on strong branches close to the main trunk, pulling other, lighter branches toward them to get at the fruit. When it has found a well-stocked tree, the spectacled bear does not bother to climb down, but instead builds a huge nest from broken branches and twigs and just goes to sleep in the tree tops.

Indian sloth bears have a strange way of feeding in trees. They have long, curved claws with which they hold onto the branches while hanging upside down, like its namesake, the South American sloth. These claws are also useful for hooking down branches that are otherwise out of reach of the bear's jaws.

Trees can be an important place of safety. When bears feel threatened they often clamber up the nearest tree. Adults usually only climb when they are challenged by bigger bears, but cubs can be attacked by a variety of other animals. Being small they can climb high into the canopy, where their heavier enemies cannot reach.

Despite their size, most bears are swift and agile climbers. Once they have reached the safety of the tree-top, young bears stay there until their mother calls them down. Using their sharp claws, grizzly bear cubs (left) can climb a tree in just a few seconds.

12

Bears and Man

Paddington, Rupert and Winnie-the-Pooh are cuddly and friendly characters, but in reality bears are often short-tempered and should be treated with caution, as they can be very dangerous. Indian tribes in America and Siberia once worshipped grizzlies as gods. When a bear died they put its skull in a holy place and prayed for the everlasting happiness of its spirit.

Although most bears are strong enough t to injure or even kill humans, they are usually timid. They only attack if they feel threatened or, even worse, if their cubs are threatened. Most will go out of their way to avoid humans, with the exception of polar bears, which will hunt man if they are hungry. Experienced travellers make plenty of noise when they pass through grizzly bear country, putting bells on their rucksacks and even singing to let the bears know that they are approaching.

Many people have tried to keep bears as pets by capturing them as cubs. Hand-reared bears can be very friendly and playful for the first few years, but as they get older they become unpredictable. The small, timid sun bears are sometimes kept as pets by locals, but even these have to be returned to the wild once they are fully grown.

"Dancing" bears used to be a common sight in fairs all over Europe. They were trained from an early age to stand on their back legs and shuffle about to music. To stop them possibly attacking the audience, the bears wore leather muzzles, and sometimes their teeth and claws were removed. Fortunately, dancing bears are now a thing of the past, and in fact bears are not even as common in zoos as they used to be, because their huge appetites make them expensive to feed.

Bear hunting was once a very popular sport. Their meat was eaten and the fur was made into clothes and boots. Theodore Roosevelt, President of the United States of America at the beginning of the century, was a keen hunter. One day he spotted a bear cub and, instead of shooting it, he said he couldn't kill anything that "looked so cute." Roosevelt was known as Teddy to his friends and, from that day, toy bears have also been known as "teddy bears."

In the Middle Ages, every town fair had dancing bears (facing page left). The animals led miserable lives and many died of neglect as they traveled around the country. Now that it is a protected species, the future for the polar bear (facing page right) is looking bright. Unfortunately, this protection does not apply to all bears, and many are still shot or caught in traps (above) to die in great pain.

13
The Future

Bears are an ancient group of animals; fossil remains show that bears and their relatives have been in existence for almost twenty million years.

Before man started using tools, fully grown bears had no enemies, but from the first days of spears and traps, bears became a hunting target. Farmers killed them to protect their livestock, and in many countries there was a reward for killing a bear. They became extinct in Britain nine hundred years ago, and this story is more or less the same throughout the world. In America there used to be about 100,000 grizzlies, but now there are probably less than 600. In Europe there are tiny groups of bears living in a few national parks, but their numbers are so low that they cannot survive much longer.

Most bears are now protected by law and cannot be killed or trapped without a license. Every year poachers kill a small number, but the biggest danger facing bears is the destruction of their habitat. As humans take more and more land for building and farming, the wilderness areas slowly disappear, and then the bears and other wildlife are left with smaller habitats that shrink more each year.

Several years ago conservationists realized that some bears were becoming rare and they tried to help. There was a worldwide ban on the sale of live sun bears and Asian black bears, and it was also made illegal to buy or sell their skins without a permit. Twenty years ago the polar

There are always problems when bears come into human territory. If the bears are to survive we have to learn to live with them. Where bears are under threat, they are being trapped and moved (above left) to areas where they have a better chance of survival.

---

bear was in real danger of extinction from over-hunting. An agreement was signed by all the countries that made up the polar bears' territory that gave full protection to the bears and allowed only a small number to be killed. Hunting from aircraft and speedboats was completely banned, and bears in winter dens and females with cubs were given extra protection. Before long, the plan started to work and now the population of polar bears is increasing.

The polar bear project should be an example to all countries. The American black bear is the only species that is surviving in good numbers. The other six species are all *endangered* to some extent, but with just a little considerate planning, all seven species could be saved for the future.

Glossary

AQUATIC ANIMAL – an animal that spends most or all of its life in water.

CAMOUFLAGE – colored fur or skin that helps an animal to remain hidden in its environment.

CARNIVORE – an animal that kills and eats other animals.

CLOUD FOREST – mountain forests that are often covered by low cloud, making them damp and misty most of the time.

ENDANGERED SPECIES – a species that is becoming rare and one day die out completely.

ENVIRONMENT – an animal's surroundings; not only the land, but also the weather and temperature.

EXTINCT – a species that has died out everywhere in the world – for example, dinosaurs.

HABITAT – the natural home of an animal.

HIBERNATION – the process of sleeping throughout the months of winter.

INCISOR TEETH – sharp, flat teeth in the front of a mammal's mouth, used as a cutting edge.

INSULATION – thick fur or feathers that protect an animal from cold temperatures.

LITTER – a group of young animals born at the same time and having the same mother.

MIGRATION – the movement of animals in search of food, breeding grounds or better weather.

NOCTURNAL ANIMAL – an animal that is active at night and sleeps during the day.

OMNIVORES – animals that eat almost anything, rather than just grass or meat.

PREDATOR – an animal that kills other animals.

PREY – an animal that is killed and eaten by another animal.

SPAWNING GROUNDS – areas of water where fish and amphibians lay their eggs, usually in very large numbers.

SPECIES – a group of animals that can breed with others of their own kind, but not with any other animal.

STALKING – following or approaching stealthily, so that the prey does not sense the presence of the predator.

TERRITORY – an area of land that is home to one animal, which then drives out any other animal of its species.

Picture Credits

Maurice R. Carlisle 7 *left*, 16, 17 *top*, 30-31; John Chellman/ANIMALS ANIMALS 7 *right*; Judd Cooney 1, 13, 18 *bottom*, 22, 23 *left*, 26, 30; E. Degginger/ANIMALS ANIMALS 17 *bottom*, 19 *bottom*; David C. Fritts/ANIMALS ANIMALS 4, 12 *top*; P. Harris 5 *bottom*; Philippe Henry 24 *left*, 25; Frank Huber 9, 11; Breck P. Kent/ANIMALS ANIMALS 8, 19 *top*; Richard Kollar 28 *right*; Michael Leach 23 *right*; C.C. Lockwood/ANIMALS ANIMALS 10, 12 *bottom*; Macquitty Collection 28 *left*; McKinley Meyers/ANIMALS ANIMALS 14 *bottom*; Hugh Miles 18 *top*; Stephen Mills 21 *bottom*; Ray Richardson/ANIMALS ANIMALS 27 *top*; Wendy Shattil and Bob Rozinski 2; John Stern/ANIMALS ANIMALS 6, 7 *right*; Stouffer Productions Ltd/ANIMALS ANIMALS 21 *top*, 24 *right*, 27 *bottom*, 29; Tom Ulrich 5 *top*, 14 *top*, 15, 20.